www.finishinglinepress.com

The Other Side of the Bed and Beyond

poems by

Linda Freudenberger

Finishing Line Press
Georgetown, Kentucky

The Other Side of the Bed and Beyond

This collection of poems is dedicated to Jim, my soulmate, the love of my life, the wonderful father to our daughters, Heather and Holly, and Boompa to Joey, Nicholas and Jaxson, the one he never met.

Grief: never ends …but it changes. It's a passage, not a place to stay. Grief is not a sign of weakness, nor a lack of faith, it is the price of love. Anonymous

ACKNOWLEDGMENTS

I would like to thank my poetry mentors Sylvia Ahrens, Katerina Stoykova,
Chris McCurry, and Leatha Kendrick for guiding my writing. "Communion"
was published in 2021 Literary Accents, Katerina Stoykova, editor. "Gingkoes
in my Life" and "Clancy" were published on the Highland Park Poetry
Facebook page. "The Other side of the Bed" was published in Workhorse
magazine 2022 The Yearling. My writing group, Lubrina Burton, John
Campbell, Carolyn Martin, and Rosemary James were very encouraging to
me to complete this book.

Publisher: Leah Huete de Maines
Editor: Christen Kincaid
Cover Art: Linda Freudenberger
Author Photo: Kevin Nance
Cover Design: Elizabeth Maines McCleavy

Order online: www.finishinglinepress.com
also available on amazon.com

Author inquiries and mail orders:
Finishing Line Press
PO Box 1626
Georgetown, Kentucky 40324
USA

Contents

Communion

After the day
we scattered
your ashes
in angry, rough
waters of Maui

A green sea turtle
beckoned me away
from the others in the bay

Enchanted
by his mossy
green shell
and sassy way

I followed

He became You
engulfing me
with peace
embracing me
with love

We journeyed
together again
a parting gift
curving your head
over your shell

Checking to see if
I followed
we swam in unison
me trailing by two feet

My mask filled with water
I popped up for air
you disappeared!

You safely herd me
back to the boat

where the others
aware I was missing
prepared to alert Coast Guard lined the deck
 with shouts of "Linda"
 pulling me back.

But Linda

I was the one who was supposed to take care of you."
He looked me in the eyes head on and spoke these
words in the elevator five minutes after our world
collapsed hearing the doctor say, "It's stage IV cancer."

The Night We Met – Feb. 1, 1973

Linda
Jim

.

I walked into the dark disco dragged by my brother and his fiancé as they tried to pry me away from moping for yet another lost love. Smoke and sweaty bodies poured in. **She gingerly walked in wearing a tight knit sweater revealing her subtle curves with long brownish blond hair brushing her shoulders. Her downcast eyes told me she was new to the scene chaperoned by a couple. I zeroed in before someone else plucked this pearl.** You came from behind with a gentle tap on my shoulder. **"Wanna dance?"** "Sure!" I answered taking another sip from Kahlua and cream for fortitude.

You held me close as "Killing me Softly" sung by Roberta Flack filled the air. Your embrace was gentle, holding me as if I was a precious crystal vase ...no grinding your hips into mine allowing me the space I needed. How did you know? **Her demure half smile drew me in. I loved when she cast those dark lashes towards the floor. I could touch and hold her since it was a slow dance. A sultry sad song with a beat which eased our hips in a side sway. Scent of light flowers filled my nostrils. Nothing heavy handed or bold about this girl.** I caught a whiff of citrusy, manly English Leather cologne on your cheek lightly caressing my cheek. Your wooly sweater tickled my chin. Gently we swayed to the music. Feelings stirred. You made me feel safe. **She let me lead her in the crowded room with her head on my shoulder baby breaths in my ear. Her body was soft, no tight muscles or bones protruding. I felt strong and masculine.**

You found us a tiny table. Teetering knees to knees, you bought me another White Russian as you sipped bourbon. I gazed into your blue gray eyes hidden behind broken dark framed glasses taped at the bridge. **Her greenish brown eyes gave me full attention. Guarded by her posture she sat perched on the chair searching for her friends. He was her big brother and his fiancé. Her drink of choice was a mellow Kahlua and cream. So, fitting.** You spoke of your dreams of being a chef on your way to the CIA. I thought, "Man this guy is cocky! Picking up chicks with those dorky glasses! So confident and knows what he wants.

I didn't let her get away. I asked to drive her home. She spoke to her brother. I let you drive me home in your souped-up, Pontiac Firebird. We made a date to go to your favorite restaurant, the Distlefink on Monday, a place you used to work for in the country, a German inn. You said wear a pretty dress it's a reservation only upscale place.

I had to move fast because I was leaving in the spring for culinary school miles away in another state. This girl was a catch, and I couldn't let her escape. Tenderly I kissed her. Our lips met for our first kiss.

Send me a sign

In the early days I would beg for traces of you.
You obliged my yearnings with
a hummingbird hovering midair above the
crimson geranium on the porch - a first!

My orchids waved with no breeze as I paid
bills at the kitchen table

I am always under the watchful eyes of
Clancy our therapy dog who crossed over to
an emothional support role instinctively
knowing the need. Following instructions
from you I'm sure.

The day after we scatter your ashes
In the waters of Maui you gave me a
Magical journey as I snorkeled with
a special green sea turtle.

Your voice fills my ears when Iam most
unaware.

Special songs suddenly pop
from the radio.

I still ask for signs and got
One that stays.
Your distinctive flared nostrils grace
Jaxson's face.
He is the grandson you never met.
The one born sixteen months after.

My heart leaps every time.

I Don't believe In ghosts

But explain to me the sights and sounds:
Muffled voices heard at odd hours in an empty house
Footsteps in a vacant upstairs room where you
spent countless hours at your desktop
The look of recognition in our Clancy's eyes
over my head and beyond my gaze
Our song that mysteriously comes on the car radio
when the loss is keen
A warmth that encircles me at random moments
My first and only sighting of a hummingbird
hovering midair sucking nectar from our crimson geranium
No explanation needed Babe, I know you're checking in.

Primed with Percocet Post Surgery

Propped with pillows in my bed
Primed with Percocet post-surgery
You flashed across the bedroom mirror.
Hazy from the Percocet
I pushed it away
But wondered
Was it really you?

Weeks later no longer
Primed with Percocet
You appeared in the bathroom mirror
Wearing your favorite olive-green fleece
This time I knew-
 You were just checking in on me.

Filling his shoes

was never my plan
but it was the only
One that fit my brace.

Limelight

Never wanting a spotlight
Shining his way
He chose behind the scenes
Even at the end
Gathered his family
And then sent them home
Quietly slipping
away before dawn
Alone
in that hospital bed.

It's the Normal things

The silence is deafening:

Gone is your music and blaring TV
No more pounding your thighs to the beat in sync
with the car radio

Brewing coffee gone
Car puttering in the driveway gone
No more snoring on the sofa as the TV drones

Opening those too tight jars for me
Slicing and dicing as sous chef to my cheffing
Shuffling gait as you swagger by my side cloaking my shoulders

Hearing your smoky voice whisper "Babe"
Letting the microwave beep till I thought it would yell "I'm done"
Doing your goofy beaver dance as you sparkle

Trashing the living room as you marathon pack for treasured scuba trips
Turning off lights like crazy leaving me to trip in the dark
Which is what I am doing now without you.

Uncharted Waters

Huddled at water's edge
I cradled you in my arms
angry ocean waves
knocked me down
"No!" I screamed as your remains were swept away.
Chris lunged for the canister.

I could not part with you…not yet.

Envisioning peaceful water to release
You, one of those kumbaya moments
instead an angry wild ocean
swallowed us both
but Chris rescued us.

Nothing went as planned.
My blood sugar bottomed out
delaying our private family ceremony.
I prepared a eulogy for you again,
different from the public memorial.
No one else spoke.

Roaring waves scared Joey
as he climbed in his daddy's arms
Away from me…
they all stood on the shore watching
except for Chris
Two years prior losing his mom
he understood.

Our Hawaiian leis floated back to shore
Wilted and straggly.
Later I learned it was illegal to release
ashes on the shores of Maui.
A boat was required 100 feet out.

Earlier opening the canister of you in the room
I learned you had been violated
at the airport…
someone had broken your seal.
Honey I'm sorry…I failed you.

OK, I fucked up

"You need to check the garage door. Someone rammed into it
when we were out."His eyes narrowed. His mouth became a
thin tight line. **"I don't need to. I was tired and hit Drive
instead of Reverse. Ok I fucked up!"**

"Why would you surface so fast? You were not being a good
mentor to Chris, a new Scuba diver watching your every
move. You could have gotten the bends!" His eyes narrowed.
His lips became a thin tight line. **"Ok, I fucked up!"**

"Did we drive through Maryland yet?" **"Maryland? We're
supposed to go through Maryland?"** "Didn't you listen to
the GPS? Where are we?" **"Well she quit talking and I kept
driving."** "OMG we're 2 hours in the wrong direction!"
"Ok, I fucked up!"

"You'd better pull over the cop has his lights on. I-80 is not
a place to speed. He's at my window ...open it!" **Damn it
I can't find the switch to unlock it in this new car!"** His
eyes narrowed. His mouth became a thin tight line.
"Ok, I fucked up!"

This was our signal. No more questions, comments, remarks!
Nada, Nada! Took us many years of discussions, arguments,
altercations, disagreements, tiffs, spats, whatever you call
then. We finally arrived after many years. It came down
to body language and four words. **Ok, I fucked up!**

Broken

How do I fix it?
The unmeshing of two lives
pulled apart by sudden death
neither of us prepared for that final
till death do us part goodbye.

How do I fix it?
You moved on to the next life
without me.
We had our own jobs and interests
and were empty nesters.
But you were always there
My rock, my buffer, my lover.

How do I fix it?
Finding a new identity this late in life
Never occurred to me there would be
a gaping hole to fill, a broken psyche
a loneliness that swallows me like
 Charlie the barracuda scooping
plankton with the night divers.

How do I fix it?
Jim, you tell me
You were the fixer betwixt us.

I want…

more time

to swim cerulean seas with you
among schools of blue tang, rainbow
parrot fish crunching coral, barracudas
brushing our thighs, sea grass luring us deeper.

more time

to climb high above the jungle canopy
then zip from platform to platform
feeling invincible as the wind buzzes
past, our ears, sights below appear miniscule.

more time

to float along the meandering Seine
lined with views of the City of Light
glimpses of the Eiffel Tower
picnics of baguettes, brie, and wine.

more time

to pique our palates with tasty morsels
of conch, escargot, plantains, manchego,
sauteed lionfish, French petit fours,
Czech goulash, or German brats and kraut.

more time

to hold your hand, gaze into your
pools of blue, feeling your smile
engulf and entice me with your
sense of wonder and adoration.

more time

to witness your pride and joy
as you drop to your knees
romping with our grandsons
crawling in and out of their fort.

more time

to walk side by side, leash
in hand guiding our Clancy
as he sniffs peemails marking
trees on our block.

more time

to hear your voice that serves
as my rudder on this perilous
path keeping me on course
through this life of loveliness
and ugliness.

More time to say that
Final good-bye.

Shared harm

'May our signed right to bear arms
Never blind our sight from shared harm'
—Amanda Gorman

Don't be fooled, bloodshed
 is not someone else's kid sister
 or strangers on the news.

It touched my family twice.

In 1985 my twenty-nine-year-old sister
kidnapped from a shopping mall
parking lot as she eased into her car.
Physically she survived.

Mental scars are permanent.
For her, her marriage,
her future children,
our parents, my family.

In '85 my five-year-old was
terrified a stranger would snatch
one of us. I could not take out
garbage without informing her.
For months she crawled
into our bed at night
frightened by
dreams gone awry.
Safety was not in her closet.

This June my grown
daughter was held hostage
in a two-hour lockdown at her clinic.
The vet clinic heals animals but not that kind.

I never fired one, owned one, or touched one.
Owning one may require me to kill.

No bullets were fired, the shooter escaped unscathed.
But did we?

Late Nights

are silent.
Thoughts are muted.
This is when you ooze
both alfresco and
simmer inside my pores.
Tears flow freely
no one will see
to ask
what's wrong?

He looked like Harrison Ford

or so my daughter said about her dad.
I never saw the resemblance till she pointed it out.
There are no photos of him in view at her house,
I have his photos everywhere.
Her younger sister and I share anecdotes of him.
The older one not so much.
I remember she was ten when I lost my dad.
She dearly clung to her daddy that day more
than her persona allowed.
Grief's gaping hole rips and drags at varying
speeds, times, and depths.

Darkness

Occupied by daylight
dreading the night
sleep eludes me
for thoughts of he

No dream
to unburden the ache
to relive the give and take
of our coffee and cream

Blackness invades my sleep
shortchanging my keep
waking to relive my loss
again and again I toss.

A year down the line
he comes to me with wine
and a dance
as I weep at a chance

To open my heart
Cracking the light.

Clancy

Ebony eyes delve deep
into mine
urging, prodding,
pleading, pressing
to be fed,
lap water from his bowl.

For an open door
releasing him to the yard
to romp in the grass
chase a ball
bark.

Simple requests for a simple life.
No iphone, no ipad, no internet
to snare him.
Connection comes with a tilt
of the head
through eyes
that window a soul
mirroring innocence.

Joy flits as a butterfly
blossom to blossom
showering loyalty and love
upon me.

Ridgeback

He was doomed.
Lacking the stripe
of backward growing hair
on his back
the ridge.
Not meeting standards.
Breeder willing
to sacrifice
for lack of perfection.
Grace from
Rescue Rhodesians
saved him.

Humans are above
such perfection
for our own
or are we?

Mollie

lines the staircase with a

    stuffed toy monkey,

        stuffed toy squirrel,

            stuffed toy puppy,

                spaced with care.

She repeats the drill

    gently carrying her babies

        in her mouth

            from her fluffy dog bed

                to proudly display

                    at the house's entrance.

Her swollen teats
drag her down
as she continues
her motherly duties
caring for babies
snatched from
her concrete cage
crying for

their puppy-mill mama.

Japanese Maple

turn intricate red
weeping lacy fingers
to touch the house, it adores.

The She Tree

Her meandering branches
cradle white crepe blossoms
lacy and stark among the stalwart
conforming pines, all towering above her.

But she was the one that shone
her beauty, her strength unique among the pines
bearing blooms each a rare snowflake
maturing to distinct forms.

her confidence led the way
while charming the eye
spawning life
and new beginnings.

Ginkgoes in my Life

Green fans flutter from summer breezes
autumn ushers fronds of saffron gold
living fossils from China
abound in parks of my life.

Leaves uniquely shaped
bring smiles
memories of Linden Street Park
adjacent to the church where we wed.

Stately tall with long trunks
whimsical petals
rippled as butterflies on the wind
in Dearborn Park where I strolled our firstborn.

Gingkoes reign
at Gratz Park as Clancy and I trace
the figure eight path before writing classes
absorbing the never-ending joy.

Chef's Hands

I worried you would get carpal tunnel or arthritis in those hands
that deftly sliced, chopped, minced as you poured a chiffonade
of vegetables into your soups. Or as you carved the tasty beef
tenderloin seasoned just right. Your garde-mange of birds
sculpted from apples and watermelons formed into baskets
amazed me along with your tomato roses. I watched you
saw ice into fish or flowers or urns to embellish buffet tables
with your art. Preparing and filling over 1,000 turkey cavities
for huge Thanksgiving buffets.

Your hands survived just fine.

It was the legs that carried you for 12 hour shifts of standing
and prepping and creating meals for many that became your
Achilles heel.

Henckel Speaks

Never been this dull
I need precision to chiffonade
mince, dice, chop at my usual
frenzied pace.

Evenly weighted down my shaft
with a thick handle to cradle her hand
she rocks me swiftly back and forth
deftly with a rhythm he taught.

Carrots and thyme attacked
on the board then scraped into the
Dutch oven marinated and simmered
aromas blend and permeate.

My blade is dull
needs to be honed and sharp
he taught her to curl her fingers
out of the path of my dance on the board.

Failed to teach her to sharpen
My steel blade with the stone and oil.
She flounders the onions, garlic, carrots, thyme
reminiscing as his sous.

Puffer

Gingerly placed in my hands
a membrane of taut ochre bands
ballooned, double your normal self
delicate and light, spotted black dorsal fin
cradled in my hands
I release you home
  watching
    your body
      slowly slim
        back to
          norm
            as you
              safely
                escape.

Shiver

In lieu of school
groups of sharks
are given the
moniker shiver.
Is it for the sleek silver
bodies that ease
effortlessly
in the sea
Hunting their prey
Mating
Playing
Cavorting?

Or does it rise
from unfounded fear
from those who
know little of them?

As I swim
with them
their exquisite
movements
draw me in
chill bumps
slither down
my arms.

The Balcony

Many summers spent looking out this balcony
suspended above the roaring creek, loblolly pines
charcoal scented picnic tables and splashing pool.
Scattered in several states our family would gather.
One week a year.

Dad in his Bermudas and polo parked on the balcony absorbing
summer sounds, forest scents and solitude. Always a book in his
lap, cut short if I joined him to give me his full attention and counsel.
Whenever I go back, he remains on that balcony.

Driving their special route from Florida to Gatlinburg
off the freeways on the narrow two-lane state roads
stopping to buy juicy fragrant peaches from a local farmer.
We returned with Mom retracing that special route the summer we lost Dad.
That summer the balcony's magic was broken by a chain smoker below us
Tainting our fresh forest bouquet.

One summer our daughter, a budding flutist trilled an impromptu concert
floating notes on treetops competing with red-bellied woodpeckers,
black-capped chickadees, and mourning doves.

Another trip my brother and I strategized how to locate
our missing daughters who were out past curfew as
Mom knotted her tissue with worry peering from the balcony.

Now the new generation of grandsons
arrive with giggles looking down
at the Roaring Fork Creek eager to catch crawdads.
First time ever a rebellious raccoon came scrounging up
our private space three floors up causing my
daughter to scream.

Next summer we will continue our legacy
Honoring those who have passed on.
Nana, Pop-pop, Dave, JP and Jim with
Barbecue, beer, cornhole, toasted some mores
To create new memories for the crawdad boys.

The Sheriff & the Outlaw #1.

Brothers of opposite molds:

the Sheriff, enforcer of rules, order, structure
OCD to the tenth degree
with a marshmallow heart.

Sheriff says, "Nana, Stop on red, Go on green."
At the drive thru window he yells plain burger, ketchup only
Not Hamburger with only ketchup."

The Outlaw ruptures rules, beats his own drum,
laughs with verve pulling your last bit of patience
along with your heartstrings.

Outlaw says, "Mommy says I can have five M&M's
when I go potty, and I only wear Toy Story pull-ups
and only 3T pajamas," as he tosses 2T over his head on the floor.

Opposite souls cuddled close as I read them tales
of sharks and superheroes
followed by the Sheriff proudly reading his primer
next come bedtime hugs and kisses.

Glimpses of that day tucked in Nana's mind
held tight
till the next showdown
with the Sheriff & the Outlaw.

Sheriff & the Outlaw Meet Junior Deputy

Peals of laughter
emerged from the Outlaw
chasing butterflies
and Citizen Canine Clancy
throughout the yard.

Outlaw wouldn't allow hugs
from Junior Deputy
who then pounced on the Sheriff
where hugs were shared.

Their Boompa watched from afar
Nana by his side.
Grinning and yearning
to wrestle
Joey, Nicholas and Jaxson
crouching
on all fours in their fort.

The other side of the bed

has been empty going on four years.
In the beginning we spooned or you curled
me under your protective wing.
As kids came and jobs pulled at us
we slept fetal back-to-back.

I cannot starfish or invade your side.
It is sacred space to me.
I yearn to hear the soft sawing
of your breath.
Still saving your space.
I cannot face the finality
of you not slipping under
the covers beside me.

Linda Freudenberger, a retired occupational therapist, lives in Lexington, Ky with her Westie, Clancy, a certified therapy dog. She began writing in 2017 after the loss of her husband of forty-two years by taking writing classes at the Carnegie Center for Literacy and Learning and enrolling in the Author Academy in 2019 under her mentor, Sylvia Ahrens, who sparked an interest in poetry. Her story, "The Call" was published in The Personal Publishing Project anthology, *Bearing Up*, edited by Randell Jones in 2018. "In the Holler" was published in the anthology, *That Southern Thing*, edited by Jones in 2020. "His Final Act of Kindness" was published in the anthology *Luck and Opportunity* edited by Jones in 2021. Her story "Bowtie Whimsy" was included in the 2022 anthology *Curious Stuff* also edited by Jones. She has three essays on the online grief site, opentohope.com. She completed a fictional novella about a teahouse that she is submitting for publication. In 2020 she participated in the yearlong Poetry Gauntlet led by Christopher McCurry writing 112 poems. Her poem, "Communion" was published in 2021 *Literary Accents*, Katerina Stoykova, editor. Two poems have been published on Highland Park's Daily online poems in 2022. "The Other side of the bed" was published in Workhorse's magazine, *The Yearling 2022*. This is her first chapbook.